Why Worry?

It may never happen.

A practical guide to confront
and stop worry

D1731880

by Marian Foss

"If they look for enlightenment and accept it, their fears vanish.

But if they hide their nightmares they will keep them.

Take off the covers and see what you are afraid of. Only the anticipation will frighten you, for the reality of nothingness cannot be frightening."

A Course in Miracles

Contents

Introduction

It seems to me the best time to start a book about Worry with everything going on in the world. If you don't feel anxious and worried about yourself, your health, your family, your home, your finance, the future, and the world, then you would probably not be reading this.

Anxiety has become the norm and yet it should not be as large a part of our lives as it is. We need to put it in its place and I hope to show how this can be done.

This book comes in three parts:

Part: 1 Worry – and how to take action.

Part: 2 Why? - The cause of anxiety and how it effects us.

Part: 3 Search for the Hero – An introduction to useful therapies and techniques.

This book is full of helpful tips, uplifting stories, effective therapies, quotes from famous people, books, websites and life affirming ideas.

Part 1: WORRY

Chapter 1. Why?

"To take arms against a sea of troubles and by opposing end them"
Hamlet - by William Shakespeare.

My mother is fond of telling a story from her childhood. She shared her bedroom with her sister and on the wall above her bed was a picture which said 'Why worry, it may never happen'.

Life happened and she married and had 3 children and never forgot that picture. She would proudly say that worry was a woman's lot. You always worry about your children. During our daily phone conversation she would always ask me how I was? And I would often say 'Don't worry about me, I'm fine' knowing that it would make very little difference to her thinking or to her emotions.

One day it occurred to me that over all these years she had got it wrong. The picture was telling her not to worry because it might not happen. It was supposed to be a reassurance. For me this was a turning point.

It may not happen.

In 1995 I had enough worry to feed an army. My long term partner killed himself leaving me destitute and ill with Rheumatoid Arthritis. The other man I had fallen for rejected me. I had a home but it was a wreck. I had a small disability income which covered the mortgage but was left with many debts. I was about as low as I could get and I wanted to know why it had happened to me?

My mother who paid for the funeral, found an article in the Daily Mail about a woman called Louise L Hay and her book 'You can heal your life'. I was introduced to new thinking about worries, about life. Positive thinking. I would have a go at anything that would help.

I started to rise from the ashes. It took time and over the next 25 years I attended lots of courses and became an Advanced Louise L Hay teacher, a Healing Breath work practitioner, a Bach Flower Practitioner and a Reiki Master. All of these helped me change my thinking and to become more positive. My health improved and I was introduced to new drugs which made a huge difference to my arthritis.

Then we had Covid and a lot of isolation for me as the drugs affected my immune system. I found myself in the Shielding group. During this time I had a lot of time alone and I started working on my anxiety, which was extreme.

I gave myself a definite routine during the day and I stuck to it. It gave me some sort of mental support.

One section of this day was reading again all the books that had changed my life. Books by Louise L Hay, Gill Edwards, Susan Jeffers and many others (all mentioned in this book). I came to a book I must have bought but had never read. It was called "Teach only Love" by Gerald G Jampolsky. In this book he started talking about a book called "A Course In Miracles" and pretty soon I knew I would have to buy it.

"A Course In Miracles" was a revelation and I started to see life quite differently. I saw my negative fears and worries as totally unreal. I had been living my life as if they were true, I believed my fantasy world.

I started looking deeply at my world, my mind, what was real and what was not, and how I was bound by these thoughts, real or not.

In "A Course In Miracles" he says that 'to give up these miscreations is the most creative and meaningful thing we can do.'

SO HOW TO DO THAT?

What is WORRY?

The dictionary says: Feel or cause to feel anxious or troubled about an actual or potential problem. (verb)

What is the difference between anxiety and worry? Apparently anxiety is more constant – but for this book we will just use the word 'worry'. It's the negative effect on our lives we are going to address.

Worry can stamp down on our happiness, including events we were looking forward to.

Worry can lead to stress. It can all pile up on you, there is so much to do! There is so much to worry about!

Some people like some stress, it keeps them motivated but at other times it can be overwhelming. So worry can lead to stress.

Let's start with worry full on. Does worry start almost before you are awake? It tells you all the things that must be done during the day?

Then it might tell you how badly you have done at something. Or how ugly or fat you are. How you have upset someone, what will they think?

All the awful things that may fill your day.

It's an endless list of negative thoughts of You Must/Should, Don't Forget and What if?

WE WORRY – but WHY?

And what do we WORRY ABOUT?

Feeling Guilt

Why haven't..... rung me?

Do they hate me?

What will others think of me?

What are they thinking?

Feeling Abandoned

Feeling Inferiority

I look so fat and ugly.
Am I wearing the right cloths?

If only I was younger, I used to be popular

My Worry

Feeling Needy

If only I could find the right man/woman everything would be OK

What if I get ill? I am sure something is wrong

Do you remember all those stupid things you did? You're stupid

Feeling Bad

8

It's worth making a list of what we worry about. Maybe a few from the diagram above like our life, our health, finances, what people think of us, our weight, our children, family, friends, what the neighbours might think, the future, the past, the world.

I would suggest here that you pick one, make it as personal as you can, (maybe don't try to fix the world yet.)

Then I want you to make a list of all of your worries connected to your chosen worry. I find a spider chart useful and fun like the diagram above.

It's important to get it down on paper. Don't just think about it, otherwise it can remain just a thought. Seeing it on paper makes it more real. Then you can look at, study and digest it. You are taking action.

Your are doing something for yourself, for a better life and that is important. Worry is a non stop thought and we are going to try to replace it with something positive and productive.

 Looking at worry is important but after seeing comes action and then understanding.

Spider Chart

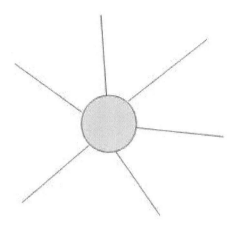

Put your worry in the center and then add as many worries about it as possible. Try and fill the page. Now I want you to put your worries into some sort of order.

One column should be FACTS – things that are true.

The other for IMAGINED WORRY.

Then what ACTION you can take.

FACTS – IMAGINED - ACTION

So we must try to separate the fact from the fiction – even though it might feel real is it?

Your mind is immensely powerful and creative.

In fact you have the freedom to choose what thoughts you put in your mind, be it worry filled or not.

You can make charges.

Your don't have to live in fear.

One of the best thing I have done is to be able to Change My Mind.

I have changed almost all the things I thought and believed particularly about anger and blame and it feels good.

Positive thinking has changed my life yet anxiety can still be present. It's a matter of how you think about it.

If you get caught up in worry or if you separate and look at it objectively. It's a continuous journey.

I think what has helped me the most is my commitment to change by taking action. Focusing on the solution not the problem. The only way to make a change is to change.

FACT: These are True and we can deal with them.

Taking action is important. Put these facts down in the table above. Look things up on the internet or go to the library, ask what can I do?

Ask questions.

At this point I would suggest you buy yourself a notebook to write down your answers, so you can look back and remind yourself the actions you are going to focus on.

If it is an illness study as much as you can about it, it is helpful to know what you are up against for instance.

It is always good to look at the positive side where people have succeeded in healing themselves. And you would be surprised to know that there are quite a few.

Taking action should always be positive.

What you understand you can deal with.

IMAGINED: Put those too in the next column.

This kind of worry cannot be pinned down.

Maybe it will happen, maybe it won't. But it keeps nagging regardless.

It is interesting to see how much is imagined and how our imagination can go overboard. Once it is out of control it can effect our whole body and our world.

These fears usually live in the future yet we have an amazing ability to go back in time and find it there too. We compare ourselves with others, what happened in the past, what we see on TV and we believe it.

Shadow figures in the past seem real but the past is gone and has no power over us. We may hold on to these shadows with anger and justification.

What if? If we start in on this we are not living in the present moment and have lost touch with life and Your power lies in the present moment, only there you can take action.

We can imagine things visually in a creative way and that is essential for every day life. However it can easily get out of control and turn to imagined worry. Visualisation is creative and productive, but worrying about what the children or the neighbours for instance are up to IS NOT REAL.

It is in your imagination ONLY.

ACTION: Fill this section out straight away or once you have done some study. It is important to make sure that these actions are possible, achievable. That you can do it and will do it. Taking action is the most important part when making changes and conquering worry in life.

YOU CAN CHANGE WORRY to A POSITIVE OUTCOME.

You have a creative mind, that is where your strength lies.

So your imagined WORRY is actually a LIE.

IT IS NOT REAL.

These things we fear rarely come true, or at least not in the way we imagine.

So WORRY IS A FALSE STATE OF MIND.

WORRY straddles past and the future blocking out the present, the now.

THESE FEARS ARE NOT REAL.

It was a huge moment for me when I first realized that what I had been worrying about was not real or true. It was only a figment of my imagination. That I could be free of all of this worry just by focusing on the present and what practical action I could take.

We are not talking here about facing fears – the present fight and flight mechanism. Because the only real power lies in the present moment. So we are talking about fear when we worry in our imagination but we believe and act as if they were real. Worry is associative, it goes from one idea to another usually leading us down into despair and doom. This worry stops us doing the one thing we need to do – TAKE ACTION.

ACTION is the only thing we can do – everything else is imagined.

We are in control of our lives and can take action.

It is impossible for instance if we worry about others for we cannot control them even if they are our children, or partner they are their own person. You could ask yourself here.

How is this helping the other person?

We all like to feel that we are coping with life (even if we aren't,) so worry for others can be counter productive. Try and trust in them as being well and capable. If you can't then consider, what can I do to help? Put it into action, things that may help. You will never know unless you ask?

We are all caught up in our own mind with our own worries. It could be useful to share.

This kind of worry can be particularly destructive. The type that go round and round and go nowhere. The answer is to repeatedly tell ourselves that this is not real – our thoughts are from our imagination not a FACT.

Questions to ask yourself:

Is this worry helping me in any way?

Is this worry helping others at all?

Is this something I am repeatedly worrying about?

Does this worry stop me from taking action?

If I took action would this dispel my fears?

Why haven't I?

Deal with FACTS and take ACTION.

FOCUS ON THE SOLUTION NOT THE PROBLEM

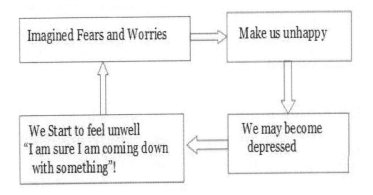

In Diving we call this the Incident Pit. Something small, a niggle or worry, something goes wrong, we lose track of the present, and pretty quickly it can build and lead to something much worse. Here again we are worrying about something that possibly has not yet happened. Worry and Fear Is in the future, in fact it does not exist.

How it can affect our body

Fear is always in the future yet it grips us in the present. We back this up with things that have happened in the past and things we have seen happening to others.

We may get ill and then becomes obsessed with the body and sickness. We see terrible consequences. We get hooked on these thoughts keeping the whole thing going – concentrating on it.

It's not real however – IT IS JUST A THOUGHT. Hang on a minute my body might be ill! It's the time to look at what is True and what is False.

Worry cannot hurt you unless you believe in it.

Worry finishes when you take control of it.

Dictionary: Sanity – the ability to think and behave in a normal and rational manner. Sound mental health.

Insanity – Doing the same thing or thought over and over and expecting a different result. - Albert Einstein.

I would define it as worrying about an event repeatedly that never actually happens yet keeping it going regardless; believing that worrying enough about it will bring it about.

Chapter 2: Beliefs

It is what we believe about life, about ourselves, the world, which keeps us as we are.

As small children we start to get our beliefs from others around us, our carers. We soak them all up like a sponge. Others beliefs become ours and we rarely think about them for the rest of our lives.

For instance if your mother had been a worrier then it is likely that you may be the same. We learn from life as we go along. It's learnt behavior. Possibly we see no need in change until something does not fit into life any more and is causing pain or mental strife. Time to make changes.

For Instance:

How do you think about yourself?

Is what you think now helpful in your life or do you put yourself down?

Could your life be improved by being more positive?

A change in perception about who and what we are in a positive way can bring about a huge change for the better.

What we think of ourselves is only a reflection of who we are.

We believe what others tell us – be they truth or lies.

Is it time to question this and see if they are actually true.

We believe our thoughts which we rarely change be it true or false.

It is easy to change our beliefs because it is just a thought but do we try?

We all have wonderful creative minds but do we praise it?

Changing beliefs can change life for the better, and here are some new beliefs for you to think about:

I CHANGE MY BELIEFS WITH EASE

I ALWAYS SUPPORT MYSELF

I PUT MYSELF FIRST

I AM CAPABLE

I AM ALWAYS DOING THE BEST THAT I CAN

I LOOK AT MYSELF IN A POSITIVE LIGHT

I FOCUS ON SOLUTIONS AND A POSITIVE OUTCOME

WHATEVER HAPPENS I CAN HANDLE IT.

Living Inside Out

So much of life we live on the outside of ourselves. We worry about our appearance, our homes and children and what they look like. We worry what others might think and worry about. We worry about the world and how it will affect us. Yet we take little time to think about our soul and our emotions.

When we get sick we start to think about the inside but we try to put that aside by looking at outside for help from others- the Doctor, from drugs or drink hoping to forget about inside.

We judge each other by our looks and this divides and isolates us even more.

But inside is where all the interesting things happen. How we feel, our emotions which direct our lives. And our spirit, who we really are, the real you. By living on the outside we are only half a person not the wonderful whole human being.

The conversations we have are generally about outside. How we look, what we are up to, about our job, what we did last week. We rarely talk about the inside, in fact talking of our emotions is generally frowned on and not encouraged. We may even feel our life has no meaning because of this. You would be wrong. There is so much more to life and so much to know about yourself.

HAPPINESS COMES FROM WITHIN

Inside is you. You are not your job, your children, your home. You are much more and you deserve a positive and happy life.

The idea of cleansing the soul came to me when I started looking inside.

I knew of the ego (Part 2) but not really the overall role it played in my life. Thanks to this I have built quite a new person inside, or is it the real person I have returned to? If I can so can you!

Starting to listen to the person inside is a good start.

How do I feel?

What would I like out of life?

Am I satisfying the person inside?

Or could life be so much more?

It's worth taking time to consider, am I happy with my life?

How would you like to be?

INSIDE

happy, loving, caring, joyous, self confident.

OUTSIDE

successful, popular, attractive, fearless, content.

As a human it's wonderful to think that we have the possibility for all of this if we are balanced inside and out. Without our emotions and the ability to express them we are only half a person and worry can destroy all of this.

Yet we all have emotions – so we all have great possibilities.

Be confident and know that you are unique, there is no one else like you.

Jung suggests that when a stream is obliged to run underground, it inevitably carries in its current not just mud but also precious stones!

Negative vs Positive

Our inner voices are either negative or positive. Any voice who tells us we can't do something, or puts us down we remember. This sinking feeling.

I remember at school being told off and the sinking feeling in the pit of my stomach. It's there that things start to get to our emotions negatively, here worry goes to work. At this point we have a chance to big ourselves up, stand up emotionally in a way, as possibly we never did.

BE POSITIVE.

Strangely we seem to listen more to the bad stuff than those who compliment, praise or give us a kind word.

Once we recognize it we can change it.

TRY IMAGINING POSITIVE OUTCOMES.

YOU ARE THE THINKER NOT THE THOUGHT.

Don't put yourself down if most of your thoughts are gloom laden we need to recognise it, to understand how we live with it and how to change it.

Our aim here is to get something good to come out of any situation. A winning situation. (see win-win in Part 3)

Recently I had a routine appointment at the Optician. My family were coming to lunch and I didn't want to be late but things started badly as he was overrunning.

As things went on he became more and more concerned with my eye pressure and I became more tense and frightened. By the end of the session he wanted me to go straight to hospital. I came home to lunch in a terrible state and had a night before the hospital would take me in.

Over night I thought 'this is a good opportunity to prove if my ideas work' So I sat down and worked it through. I felt fine, I had no problems seeing. But I saw myself in the future with cataracts and blind from Glaucoma. I knew that this was just a fiction, the opticians opinion and not confirmed by a Doctor. Not necessarily true and I told myself this. I knew that whatever happened I could handle it. I told myself quite firmly that I did not need to be reminded of the bad stuff, NOT REAL just possibilities. It was just fantasy because I didn't know what was going to happen, but I worked hard during the night to see a POSITIVE OUTCOME. The Doctors were here to help me.

Next day the Doctor confirmed that my eyes were OK if not a bit high in pressure and gave me an appointment for 6 weeks time.

Several weeks later the Specialist confirmed that my eyes were free of glaucoma just that I had thick cornea.

It was an unexpected worry yet I got a lot from it. For me it was a winning situation. I had been able to sleep quite well. I had coped and not been stressed when talking to the doctor. I was relaxed when the nurse gave me the pressure test so my levels were lower. I had spent quality time with my brother who took me to hospital

I had met some nice people and spent time enjoyably. I had proved that my ideas worked when not overcome by worry. I felt positive about the whole event, I was relaxed at the hospital when I met the Specialist and able to ask questions and confer as one human beings to another, knowing that she was trying to help me. Whatever happened I handled it! For me it was a Win-Win through positive thinking.

Positive thinking or Affirmations is no new idea, the alternative self-help books are full of them. I struggled with Affirmations for a long time and came to the conclusion that an Affirmation was JUST A THOUGHT, a positive thought.

Something has to replace negative thoughts and a positive thought is preferable to misery and unhappiness.

Good/Positive thoughts should be in the present tense, and always positive like 'I AM HAPPY' not 'I would be happy if I feel better.' (see Part 3 for more information)

A Louise L Hay expression here which might help and I have found invaluable:

IT'S ONLY A THOUGHT AND A THOUGHT CAN BE CHANGED

Chapter 3: Creative Thinking

How to live with creative thinking? It's no problem, it's just a matter of thinking differently.

Brain storming your options.

Brain storming, giving yourself options, as many as you can think of.

Be creative however mad it might seem.

Small successes give us confidence.

Something good will come out of it.

I first heard of WIN-WIN from a best-selling writer called Susan Jeffers PhD, who wrote 'Feel the fear and do it anyway'®. This idea is to get something good out of any situation, win-win, (see Part 3) even if things go wrong you can learn from it. It takes a while to learn especially when bad things happen but when you look for a good outcome you will find it. Pat yourself on the back.

Louise L Hay talks about creativity saying that "You don't need to write a novel or do a painting to be creative. Every cell in our bodies are constantly creating. And we are creative in our minds with our responses and emotions towards every day things. We are creative every moment including our attitude about ourselves. A powerful gift is our imagination. Use it wisely to see good things happen to self and others.'" Quote from 'Trust Life' Published by Hay House on 2nd Oct 2018

If you look ahead into the future for instance try and look at good outcomes, having a better day, seeing the world as a better place where we all live in happiness and love.

There is no point in saying 'This will never happen, ain't it awful', that's not being creative.

Look at possibilities.

There is always more than one way to look at an outcome.

Try looking for the best in life, in others. For we are all human regardless of what appears on the outside.

Give it a try! Look for the good outcome.

Life is a Road Trip

Recently I visited a friend in Cornwall. I decided to drive by myself despite feeling anxious about the trip. So I decided to stop half way.

By the time I reached my Hotel I was in a state and my stomach in knots, an IBS* flare up. *(Irritable bowel syndrome)

At one in the morning I woke in a complete panic. I realized I was half way. I looked at the way I had come and how far I had to go tomorrow. I tried to calm myself, be logical and know that my imagination was making things worse. I got up and had a peppermint tea and eventually got back to sleep.

By the time I reached my friends the next day not much has changed. I was still anxious so went for a rest. Then I had the light bulb moment and I got up and made a spider chart.

Looking for solutions and facts, not imagined ones. I saw quite clearly that I could cope with the facts presented and what I could do about it.

My anxiety lifted and my stomach returned to normal almost instantly.

Things were going well despite the weather until on Wednesday my friend came down with Covid and I packed and set off home, canceling the hotel half way. I thought I must get home in case I come down with it. I knew that action had to be taken and so at this point I worked out:

The ONE STEP AT A TIME method:

Check the route

Get into the car

Start driving

If you find yourself worrying about the future of the trip bring yourself back to now, the present. Eyes on the road, look at other vehicles. Do not focus on timing it does not matter when you arrive. Go with the flow, stop when you feel like it. One step at a time and you are safely home and dry.

I drove all the way and reaching home elated and calm. I knew I had the energy and I didn't care what time I got there. I was willing to do it.

It was not a straight forward drive. At Bodmin the A30 was closed and I got lost twice. Yet here I was, tired but invigorated. My stomach has been fine ever since.

I came to various conclusions.

Try and organize your life and events where things DON'T MATTER.

For instance if you are going somewhere try and leave early so it does not matter what time you arrive. If needs be say you may be late, giving yourself time so you are not anxious.

Try cutting down on doing too much.

Be willing to FAIL so things don't matter so much.

Be willing to cancel trips, lunches, meetings etc:- if you are too stressed about them.

NOTHING IS WORTH A LIFE OF ANXIETY

Be a looser, a drop out, don't worry about what if!

Do nothing and be happy.

BREAKING THE CHAIN.

So why do we worry?

Because we know that life is unpredictable and bad things can happen. We look for the worst things that we can imagine.

Negative thinking is associative. One thing leads to another and pretty soon you are at the bottom of the pit.

The way to break this chain is with positive ways:

Recognize it

Confirm it's not real

Put something positive in it's place – (see Part 3)

Think creatively – brain storm your options

Know that you are better than this

Don't criticize yourself – (we all do it.)

Take action

Learn from it

Recognize it when (and if it comes up again)

Look for a positive outcome

Focus on the solution (not the problem)

Q: Now you know that most of your fears and worries are imagined are you ready to let them go?

A: Yes. Why would you want to keep hurting yourself?

We have to be willing to let the old thoughts go which cause us worry and fear and are not real. We, like small children have been busy frightened ourselves. Here are some affirmations for you to think about that might help:

I SEE MY ANXIETY NOW AS SOMETHING TO RELEASE

I FREE MYSELF FROM OLD THOUGHTS AND EMOTIONS THAT DON'T SUPPORT ME

I HAVE THE POWER TO MAKE CHANGES

IT'S ONLY A THOUGHT AND A THOUGHT CAN BE CHANGED

I ALLOW MYSELF TO BE HAPPY

WHATEVER HAPPENS I CAN HANDLE IT

I FOCUS ON POSITIVE SOLUTIONS AND OUTCOMES

THERE ARE MORE THAN ONE ANSWERS TO QUESTIONS

I AM CAPABLE AND STRONG

I AM ALWAYS SAFE, IT'S ONLY CHANGE

I GET THE BEST OUT OF EVERY SITUATION

I CAN DO IT!

CHANGE YOUR THINKING,

CHANGE YOUR LIFE

Part 2: Why?

Chapter 4: Childhood Onward

'All the world's a stage, and all the men and women merely players.'
William Shakespeare

Louise L Hay always said that we are unique. "Nature never repeats itself. Since time began there have never been two snowflakes alike or Rain drops the same. If you think about it it's pretty amazing. Our fingerprints are different, and we are different. We are meant to be different."

She says that to be like another shrivels the soul.

Quote from 'Trust Life' Published by Hay House, 2nd Oct 2018

We are unique and have come to this planet to express who we are.

So why are we trying to fit in and worrying when we don't? Why do we want to be like our peers, people we look up to? Why aren't we happy with who we are? An individual, unique.

CHILDHOOD

A baby is perfect and open to influences from everywhere. It loves and it wants to please. It will give it's all to grow and be as it's loved ones want it to be. It does not distinguish between right and wrong, good or bad. It learns this from it's peers and at this age it does not judge. It is open to everything.

Get the hang of potty training without too many problems, that is good. But possibly (as it was for me) suddenly you are being told there is something wrong with you. You are not perfect, in fact somehow you are bad, and you are doing something wrong which you don't really understand.

I remember having an 'accident' in my pants and thinking that I knew mum would be very angry. And that was to be avoided at all costs, I wanted to keep her happy.

That was my first experience of being divided that I can remember. I was no longer one unit, me, perfect and good enough. All of sudden I was thinking about my mother and how to please her. I knew I was bad for having an accident and I hid it. She would never know. Interestingly it was my first experience of worry and of hiding my emotions.

Would she find out? Would I get away with it? If I was really good would she love me again or would I be rejected?

Now I became split and took a creative decision. I created another part of me to cope with problems behind which I could hide.

The beginning of the Ego – my creation which would go on in life to help me cope with others and the World. It would go on to be so effective that I would forget who I really was, perfect and joyful in life. And this ego would go on to help and hinder my entire life.

I also realized years later that this was an amazing creation of the mind.

Just to prove how powerful we are.

Like worry it was not real. An imagined creation.

Pierre Daco – a Belgium Psychotherapist in his book 'How to interpret your dreams' suggested that: 'All Human Beings have a great future behind them.'

SCHOOL DAYS

He goes on to say: 'Education consists on suppressing that universal or spirit in every child'.

We are universal. We are the same stock and same substance as the rest of the universe. We are taught that to fit in we must cultivate characteristics similar to everyone else, which constitute our worth. Do not be unique or individual.

At school we automatically separate the children from each others and from the world that he or she inhabits.

Teachers studiously maintain this illusion that we are good/bad, stupid/ clever and we are judged on our achievements. The child becomes pigeon holed, and throughout their education this continues.

It's perfect feeding ground for the ego who throughout our education it grows to cope with what we can't cope with, judgment and criticism.

I can remember feeling desperate as a child. I was not good at school and being dyslexic didn't really understand things like everyone else. I had been put at the bottom of the class and I felt it. The ego helped me cope best I could.

As I slipped away into my imaginary world where I was safe the ego was sitting at the desk coping with the world of school.

Instead of re-appearing at the end as a free spirit we become funneled down the narrow tube of education. We assume the shape of the tube that produces us and so come out the other end like millions of others. We have been given our place in life. Set up, if you like for the future. Good or bad, right or wrong. We now believe that this is who we are. We emerge trying to be better, separate than others.

This is where we learn loneliness and unhappiness.

TEEN YEARS

Teenagers in bodies growing into adulthood, individuals, with raging hormones and new emotions. Due to a life time's training they may find emotions difficult to express, or are discouraged from doing so. There are no teenagers alike.

Yet here we are even more desperate to fit in. Look the same. Be in the right group, be accepted. Wear the right clothes and judge each other by our appearance. The right brand or else.

We are busy looking outside to fit in. We have forgotten who we are. And that's not surprising considering the tunnel we have been pushed down.

We have a chance here to look back at our desires and things we loved, and form our unique ideas on life. Or we can create more egos to cope with the next phase into adulthood.

Can you remember your teenage days?

How did you cope?

Was it fun or was it tough and how did your peers deal with you?

How did you feel about yourself?

One answer might be you were not happy and confused. Why did people suddenly treat you differently with lack of trust?

So the ego was formed under duress.

We felt threatened and put up a barrier to the world.

Over time we forgot who we were and the ego coped on our behalf

It could lie and cheat,

And protect us when we felt threatened

It could hide us when we felt not good enough or intimidated. Our buffer against the world

FURTHER EDUCATION

Some of us continue with our education and go to college or university. We are still getting funneled some more to come out the other end as SOMETHING not SOMEONE. A builder, an accountant, a hair dresser. Something we pin down and say 'I am a ....', this is me.

When we meet and greet others we talk about our job - 'What do you do?' Or about our mortgage, or children, or about others. As we get old we talk about our ailing body, our complaints and the tablets we take.

What we avoid is talking about who we are and expressing our emotions. For some reason this has become taboo. Even worry we keep to ourselves. It is not discussed, like sex 60 years ago.

Yet we want people to know and love us as we are. We want people to know us.

Think about our emotions

Why do we keep our feelings hidden?

Interestingly the emotions are the bridge to the soul. As long as we find emotions difficult to express we will need the ego. It is presently how we connect with the World.

Once we know how to use the ego to our advantage we will no longer believe in it. It will have no power over us and we will have the ability to use it for good.

We are actors on the stage of life and when we know that we can take life more lightly. An adventure not a trial through life. We can change and be what we like. Open ourselves to all possibilities.

Louise L Hay says, 'Life to me is an education. Every day I open my mind and heart and discover new insights, new people, new viewpoints, and new ways to understand what happens around and within me. The more I understand, the more my world expands'.

Quote from 'Trust Life', Published by Hay House, 2nd Oct 2018.

LOVE AND MARRIAGE

'I'm Worried about Jim!'

My mother used to put us to sleep in the middle of the day for a nap and we always listened to the radio. Mrs Dale's Diary was her favorite – a 50's radio soap about Mrs Dale and her family.

Jim was her husband, the local Doctor and every episode seemed to start with her worry, mostly about Jim. If she ever worried about herself it seemed unlikely, certainly it was not mentioned. The worry for others was paramount, and a woman's lot.

The programme was all about middle class values in which Mrs Dale worries about her husband and family. Firstly the women had to get the right kind of husband and the men had to try and avoid problems at work. It was all about doing the right thing, not rocking the boat, avoiding scandal with a small amount of gossip. Only romantic love was acceptable and was glorified. She held all the strings of the family but she always down play her role and boosted and controlled everyone else.

Mrs Dale gave us, in the 50's the idea of the kind of life we were expected to live. How to be good wives and carers and worry was important in this context and expected. Worry was part of the package.

The little woman did not stand up for herself. She came second to her husband. She had her role and she stuck to it. Part of her role was worrying about everyone else.

Things were dramatically to change in the 60's. Firstly we women could go on the pill and Free Love was the slogan. We went to wild raves and took drugs. But were we ready for the sexual revolution?

Slowly we were changing our world. There was no going back to Mrs Dale. Now we had new things to worry about not only our family but about our job and our place in society.

However our beliefs and memory of those 50's morals were now embedded in our subconscious. So we went for it but worried about what we had done. Where was that perfect husband? Probably not at the rave stoned out of his head! But getting a partner was essential, a vital part of life, and still is. Our dreams of the perfect partner has not changed.

ELEPHANT IN THE ROOM

Our family lived pretty much as a 50's family should. We didn't talk of sex and we did not talk of love or say that we loved each other. Emotions were taboo except anger which surfaced quite often.

It was not done and emotions were not part of our vocabulary. It never occurred to me until later that we never mentioned love.

My Father would become deeply embarrassed if someone on the TV kissed or showed emotions. We too would cringe. Any show of strong emotions were to be avoided. We lived on the outside and our emotions within was nicely hidden.
Underneath all of this was worrying particularly for my mother.

It takes a lot of energy to keep things hidden and under control. The ego has to work very hard to keep everything under control.

This was our Elephant in the Room and it was never talked about or discussed.

I had a long term non conformist relationship. On the surface not like my parents. We lived freely as an unmarried couple. No children to hold us back, doing what we wanted to do.

But we didn't express our feelings or discuss love. So we followed the same rules. These things were 'just understood'.

He was not interested in my problems and I had no one to discuss them with. I am not sure now how I would have gone about it. Talking about my emotions was something I had never done.

So when he committed suicide I cried every day for a year. It was like a dam had broken. I read about crying, I read about anger. I started to understand my emotions and express them. The more I expressed my anger the cleaner I felt inside. This was my opportunity to reach the emotions that I had not expressed. For I had become rigid from arthritis. I was so full of pain in my body I could not move and I put the two together.

Rigidity – Arthritis - Suppressed Emotions

The importance to express and understand our emotions are paramount for our health.

At Stanford University they have discovered that for women to have good health they need to talk about their feelings. For women this is more important than exercise or a good diet.

Failure to create and maintain quality personal relationships for women is as dangerous to physical health as smoking!

Our ego can spend a lot of time trying to control others, trying to organize events, know how others should live their lives and are full of suggestions of how to do it.

So Ego and worry are deeply intertwined.

We can try and control others as much as we like and worry about them but actually it may get us nowhere. Worry stops us from tackling or expressing the underlying problem which is usually emotionally based.

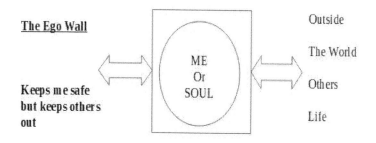

The ego is good at defense and protecting us. So when it is time to express emotions a new idea is needed. We tend to blame each other.   But while we are busy blaming others they are doing the same. It's ego against ego. Nothing will change.

Everyone is defending their wall and justifying it. After all you are attacking someone who has a similar ego wall.

Chapter 5: Making Changes

Instead of Accusation try a different approach, Assertiveness.

Assertiveness. Stand up for Change of the Individual

The need to be ME and not part of a unit, a unique individual

Assertiveness is a way of stating your own feelings in a positive way in the present tense, as attacking others and blame does not work.

Start by asking yourself: How do you actually feel?

And: What would you like to express?

If you are worried say it from your point of view. Take responsibility for your own feelings and express that. The answer is to tackle with actions (as we did with worry) in a positive way.

Learning Assertiveness is based on mutual respect. We stand up for our own interests and express our thoughts and feelings from our own point of view. What we cannot do is accuse others of things. It is based on our feelings only.

It takes a bit of getting used to but I believe it is essential to live a worry free life. If we cannot express our feelings we are only half a person, living for others and on the outside of life.

If we worry about someone else it is best to talk to them directly. Talk from your own point of view only. If you are finding something difficult that they are doing say so. What you can't say is: 'You make me feel, it's your fault,' don't blame. We are trying to stop Blame, Judgment and Humiliation which are the things that Ego likes too much.

Instead of running away from emotions try now to face the world and tackle things head on. And being positive and learning are part of the whole packaging.

Remember

YOU ARE GOOD ENOUGH EXACTLY AS YOU ARE

ASK FOR WHAT YOU WANT

ALWAYS FROM 'I' don't bring others into it.

TRY AND STICK TO IT.

NEW THOUGHTS

'We are spirits in the material world', The Police

At 19 I got myself a Guru which was fashionable at the time. What the Beatles did – so did everyone else. I stayed with him for about 6 years until he sadly died.

He kept me on track and got me through Art School when other I knew dropped out. That was a good thing for me. I had achieved something for once.

The thought then in spiritual circles was that the ego was a bad thing to be rooted out. It was an evil which stopped me becoming my true self. However hard I tried I could not rid myself or it. I cursed myself constantly and struggled on. Worse, I felt really bad about myself. Whatever about myself I didn't like always seem to come up stronger. I learnt it was called the shadow. Things I didn't want to see or worry about returned to haunt me.

Now I understand that the ego is part of me, my creation. And as long as I felt some part of me was bad I would never be happy and would worry about it. The part of me that didn't deserve any good, love and peace. After all I was not good enough however hard I tried.

Modern thought is now that we must love ourselves regardless, complete, ego and all. I prefer this modern thought, it is kinder and has the possibility of a happy life. It make us all human regardless, on the same journey, with great possibilities.

There is no escape from the ego and we shouldn't want it. It is our creation, part of us.

The way forward is:

RECOGNITION

LEARNING

UNDERSTANDING

CHANGE

Recognizing what is real and what isn't and dealing with it.

Making changes can be easy and fun, it depends how we look at it.

Climb the stairs to a better and happier life. Forgive the past and let it go.

FORGIVENESS

Louise L Hay says, 'The past has no power over me because I am willing to learn and grow. I see the past as necessary to bring me to where I am today'.

Quote from 'Trust Life' Printed by Hay House, 2nd Oct 2018.

As our ego grows from childhood we start to blame others for our problems. They have ruined our lives. We start to feel inferior and we imagine how we would get back at them, even if we never do. Then we may feel guilty about feeling angry. It all gets stored up. And like the ego it is not real. It's just a thought.

The past is gone and has no power over us. Only in our mind does it exist. (see part 3) We are surrounded by things from our past. Our home and the environment we live in. We can touch them and acknowledge that they exist but actually the past events that have affected us HAVE GONE.

So holding on to anger from the past can only do us harm. It only exists in our mind.

Here my friend Christopher Boyce an NLP Practitioner (Nero Linguistic programming) talks about his work:

"I qualified as a NLP Practitioner and that brought me into contact with people who had emotional issues that they needed help with.

With the people I worked with I tried to help them overcome some traumatic event in their life. They would always refer and recall an event that caused them to feel how they are feeling now and the suffering they had been through since the traumatic event.

I would say to them, 'I empathize with you and I understand the suffering you have encountered because of the event. But that event does not exist now. That event only exists in your mind."

Their reply was always the same, " Of course it exists, it happened to me."

I would say, "OK, let's put our coats on, we'll get in my car and I want you to take me to the event." Their reply would be, "I can't, it's gone in the past."

My reply, "But you told me it's real, and now you tell me you can't take me there, so where is the event?"

Their reply,"I get it now, it exists only in my head doesn't it."

Then they get the light bulb moment and from then onward they change their thinking."

THE PAST HAS NO POWER OVER YOU

THE ONLY POWER THE PAST HAS IS THE POWER THAT YOU GIVE IT

YOUR POWER LIES IN THE PRESENT MOMENT

Now you may see how important Forgiveness is. Without it we are stuck with the way we see the world. We may carry these worries with us for years. You are the only one who is suffering.

FORGIVENESS is a WINDOW into a NEW LIFE, into FREEDOM

If we can forgive others then we can rid ourselves of their influence in our life. We can start living for ourselves. A clean slate.

We can see things more clearly, maybe recognize why and how they reacted to us originally. We can make our own judgments about life.

The idea is to look at the past more objectively. To lose all the fear that ego creates keeps us stuck in the past, with a negative view of the future.

This is ego not you. Know the difference and you are half way there to reunite with your soul, the true you.

The ego keeps us stuck in the past and looking forward to more of the same in the future. In fact we have no idea what will happen in the future. (See part 3 for Forgiveness ideas).

After all as the past does not exist – forgiveness is inevitable.

Why hang on to something that does not exist?

EMOTIONAL CONNECTION

Dr Edward Bach the creator of the Bach Flower Remedies said: "As long as our Soul and personality are in harmony all is joy and peace, happiness and health. It is when our personalities or ego are led astray from the path laid down by the Soul, either by our own worldly desires or by persuasion of others, that a conflict arises. The conflict is the root cause of disease and unhappiness."

Sometimes when we get angry and complain to anyone who will listen we feel emotionally buoyant. We feel justified in our anger and if we have been depressed we feel better. For anger is a higher vibration in the emotional scale.

However anger not expressed can send us down again. In part 3 you will find the Emotional Ladder. It will explain how our emotions move up and down, making us feel better or worse.

Interestingly worry is about half way up the ladder. Impatience is the next rung up. So if you are worried you have a chance to move up towards hope, for hope and optimism lead to happiness and then freedom.

EMOTIONAL HEALING

About two years after my partner died I moved to Wales. It seemed a good idea and selling my house gave me a chance to be free of debts.

I discovered a massage therapist who turned out to be a great mover in my life. She told me about the Bach Flower Remedies (see Appendix 1) and suggested I look them up.

I discovered that the Bach Flowers were natural remedies made from wild flowers and could heal the emotions. Having looked at a book I discovered I needed all of them. (see Part 3)

So I set off on an adventure into new emotional territory.

The idea of healing my emotions painlessly, just by taking a few drops of water seemed too good to be true. Quite quickly I had some dramatic experiences.

I was taking Beech – for intolerance, and Chicory – for possessiveness and selfishness when I headed into town to do some shopping. On my return, putting things away I noticed that something had changed. I was stunned to discover that a whole raft of negative thinking about others had just gone. I had never really been aware how it affected my day or even that it was there when dealing with others until then. I had not really been aware of the negative thought at all until they were gone.

After that I started to study with keen interest. I then moved and started training as a Bach Practitioner.

I have put in the Appendix the 38 flower remedies with their negative and positive emotional outcome. For it's in the emotions where we make real changes. It's the positive outcome where we are heading. Once you have taken a step on this emotional ladder there is only one way to go, upwards.

YOUR LIFE

A CHANGE IN DIRECTION PUTS YOURSELF IN CHARGE OF THE JOURNEY

There are lots of things you can do to make changes:

Be kinder

Be more helpful

Look more closely at other peoples lives before criticising

Give rather than take

Abandon guilt and self abuse

Big yourself up

Look for the good side of life

Laugh more

Sing in the shower

Watch more comedy than violence

Get out in nature as much as possible

Be more loving towards yourself

If there are things about yourself you don't like change them, and trust that your future will be good. Thanks for that, and thank for your family and friends who give you a chance to see the world through others eyes.

Do less – love more.

REAL OR NOT?

As we have discussed there are many things we consider real are not. Nothing is in our control except our own lives. And that is where you must start. Knowing it is just a thought and not an event. For love not fear is the only place of peace.

The mind will do whatever we tell it to do. Give it anything, new people, new places, new studies to raise your emotional vibrations. It's up to you.

If you find music inspiring listen to it. There is so much out there about love and hope. Or look at nature in all it's glory. See the good in life and see the good in others around you. Particularly inspiring people who have achieved something you admire.

BE INSPIRED – Lift up your hearts. Lift up your spirits.

Open your mind to NEW possibilities.

You can be the person making changes.

Although we are 'spirit in the material world we need the ego. It is our creation which can cause us pain only if we believe in it. But also it is how we connect with the world, how we get on, how we express our life experiences.

Once we understand how the ego works we can use it to our own advantage. We can be an actor on the stage of the World. We have the possibility to be anything we want. We are a spirit in the material world.

We have creative minds so we can take ourselves more lightly, with more humour. We can look to see if our beliefs are valid in the light of what we learn. This way is true freedom.

Know that you are a wonderful person doing the best that you can.

Know that you are spirit.

Know that you are a truly creative being with all possibilities.

Know that you are unique and you are part of the web of everything.

There is no other person like you.

RE-CONNECTION TO HUMANITY

So what makes us human?

RE-CONNECTION TO HUMANITY
So what makes us human?

Ego is the only thing that is not essential to life and keeps us distant and apart from our fellow humans.

See others through the eyes of the soul, for connection with humanity is the way to a wonderful, peaceful and loving world.

Louise l Hay says: 'No soul has ever been harmed and therefore does not need redemption. It is our personality or ego that needs to be reminded that we are spiritual beings having a human experience, not the other way round.'

Quote from 'Trust Life', Published by Hay House on 2nd Oct 2018.

I DO THE BEST TO HELP CREATE A LOVING

HARMONIOUS WORLD

And so it is.

Part 3 – Search for the Hero

Chapter 6: Search

'Search for the hero inside yourself, Search for the secrets you hide, Search for the hero inside yourself, Until you find the key to your life.'
Quote from the band M People.

We are all on a journey through life. Good and bad things happen and we deal with them as best we can.

This section is an aid to help you on your journey. I have found all of these tools invaluable and am now able to get something good out of any event, good or bad.

In this section I have written about the therapies as well as sections like assertiveness and breathing, all of which I have found in my quest for a happy and healthy life.

When I was first diagnosed with Rheumatoid Arthritis I was working for a television company in central London. They had private medical insurance so I was referred to a top Harley Street Rheumatologist.

When I got made redundant he offered to continue to see me at Saint Bartholomew's Hospital in the City of London, knows as Barts.

I had no particular interest in alternative medicine and knew little about it and was happy to take the standard drugs prescribed. I started on the standard 'let's hit your immune system' drugs.

I remember getting terribly ill on a dive trip with my partner to Cornwall and just made it to the phone box in Penzance car park to call the Rheumatologist. "Come back" he said. So we drove back to Barts and he stopped all my drugs except an anti-inflammatory.

He suggested a new regime for me. Half of his patients were remaining on standard medication but the others he wanted to refer to the Royal Homeopathic Hospital. And so I went.

Homeopathic medicine worked for me along side my anti-inflammatory and I had many years of being fairly stable only with the occasionally flare up. I managed to continue with work and even bought a horse with my redundancy money.

This opened a door to new ideas for me. Before I had been skeptical but now I looked further into other therapies.

I had always meditated with my Guru in the 60's and after my partner died I started to look at anything that would help in my quest for health and happiness, however wacky it might seem. These next chapters I have enclosed all the things that are not only useful (not the wacky ones), but have helped me turn my life around. They are tried and tested by me.

There is no reason that they could not do the same for you too.

Paul Simon said he did not know where his songs came from. He would listen to tapes that people had sent him while driving his car and then the song would appear.

When he wrote 'Bridge over troubled waters' he was listening to gospel. When he wrote 'Graceland' he had been listening to African music. It was a big decision for him to go to South Africa on the back of that idea during the time of apartheid. Most people were against it including his record company.

He had little to lose. His previous album 'Hearts and Bones' had flopped. The relationship with his partner Art Garfunkle had deteriorated and his marriage to Carrie Fisher had collapsed.

'Graceland' became his most successful album estimated at sales of 16 million world wide. In 1987 it was the Grammy album of the Year and frequently cited as the best album of all time.

It became his greatest creative achievement. And why? Because he stepped out of his comfort zone and took a step into the unknown.

He was searching for the Hero and he found much more.

So we need some sort of incentive, some reason and desire to look for the Hero. Don't forget that you have choice. You can make decisions, it's your life. This next section will provide a lot of impetus and ideas.

Search for inspiration

Challenge your thinking

Take that first step. Spread your wings and fly.

Chapter 7: AFFIRMATIONS
or Positive Statements

Dictionary: Affirmations – the action or process of affirming something

Noun: emotional support or encouragement.

Louise L Hay says: "That she does not see thoughts as positive or negative. Thoughts are always neutral. It's the way we handle our thoughts that are either positive or negative."

So how do we change our mind?

We have to change our relationship to our mind.

And how do we do that?

Remember that we are the thinker, not the thought.

Learning to think in positive affirmations or statements.

Louise L Hay says: " Every single thought I have and every sentence I speak is an affirmation. It is either positive or negative. Positive affirmations create positive experiences and negative affirmations create negative experiences.

If I continually repeat negative statements about myself or about life, I will keep producing negative experiences.

I now raise beyond my old habit of seeing life in a negative way. My new affirmation habit is to only speak of good I want in my life. Then only good will come to me."

Quote from 'Trust Life', Printed by Hay House on 2nd Oct 2018.

Affirmations can be any statement you make. Too often we think in negative affirmations. Negative affirmations only create more of what you say you don't want. Saying, "I hate my job", will get you nowhere. Declaring "I now accept a wonderful new job", will open the channels in your consciousness to create that.

Continually make positive statements about how you want your life to be. However, there is one point that is very important in this: Always make your statement in the PRESENT TENSE, such as "I am" or "I have". Your subconscious mind is such an obedient servant that if you declare in the future tense, "I want", or "I will have", then that is where that idea will always stay – just our of your reach in the future!

I suggest you write out your affirmations in your notebook. It makes a difference putting something on paper – it means that you are serious and want to change. You have made a commitment to yourself.

Louise also suggested that you write them on post it's and stick it on mirrors and places around the house where you will see them easily. Also saying them out loud or making them into songs.

When I did the Louise L Hay course to train as a teacher we sang songs all the time and I bought the CD's. I still remember them and sing them in the shower.

Louise also suggests that when you look in the mirror you tell yourself that you love yourself. The premises of Affirmation work is to learn to love yourself. Louise says that when you love yourself you heal you life.

I found this difficult to start with when I looked in the mirror. I was always looking to see if my hair was right and I found myself telling myself how ugly and stupid I was. I also found this with putting stickers around the house. I was concerned what others might think that I had really lost the plot!

One day I came to the conclusion that it was all about HOW I FEEL ABOUT MYSELF. The post-its and notebooks were just a reminder.

Using the Affirmations have been invaluable for me. I have a string of them for various circumstances. For instance when I feel unwell I say HOW WONDERFUL MY BODY IS and I believe it.

The body is constantly healing itself. Skin keeps replacing, hair is growing, nails; it is impossible to stop this renewal unless you are in space!

Our body is constantly healing. Look how quickly a cut heals!

And when it does thank it - and that is an affirmation.

Having been ill and in pain for many years and cursing my body I finally saw the light and now I LOVE MY BODY and see how wonderful it is. I thank it for doing a good job (now that I am not giving it negative thoughts.)

Louise suggests that you take one or two affirmation and write them 10 or 20 times a day. Read them aloud with enthusiasm. Let your mind go over these affirmations all day long. Affirmations that are used constantly become beliefs and will always produce results, sometimes in ways that we cannot even imagine.

If you are struggling creating a good affirmation I would suggest that you pick a negative one and turn it to the positive.

Like: 'Why am I always worried' To: 'I live a carefree life'

The idea is to keep away from negative words so saying 'I am not worried about life' would be incorrect for we are mentioning 'worry'.

Here are some Useful Affirmations

THE PAST HAS NO POWER OVER ME – I AM MY OWN PERSON

IT'S ONLY A THOUGHT AND A THOUGHT CAN BE CHANGED

I'M A POSITIVE PERSON WITH POSITIVE THOUGHTS

I HAVE A WONDERFUL CREATIVE MIND

I CHANGE MY MIND EASILY

I AM SAFE, IT'S ONLY CHANGE

MY BODY KNOWS HOW TO HEAL ITSELF AND IS DOING SO

WHATEVER HAPPENS I CAN HANDLE IT

I AM SAFE – ALL IS WELL IN MY WORLD

I AM NOT MY PAST

I AM WILLING TO FORGIVE THE PAST AND I AM FREE

LOVING MYSELF HEALS MY LIFE

MY POWER LIES IN THE PRESENT MOMENT

I AM IN THE PROCESS OF POSITIVE CHANGE

TODAY IS A NEW AND SPECIAL DAY

I LOVE AND APPROVE OF MYSELF

I ACCEPT MY UNIQUENESS

IT IS SAFE TO LOOK WITHIN

Plenty more on these on these useful websites: www.optimistminds.com/affirmations–for-adults

www.positiveofficemationcentre.com-for-adults
www.lousiehay.com
www.healyourlife.com

Chapter 8: Assertiveness

How to Build Self-esteem

Dictionary: Confident and direct in claiming one's rights or putting forward one's own views.

The ability to express our ideas and feelings, both positive or negative, in an open, direct and honest manner.

The ability to stand up for our rights, while respecting the rights of others.

The ability to take responsibility for ourselves and our actions, without judging or blaming other people.

The ability to find compromise where conflicts exists.

All of us behave assertively at times, but when we feel vulnerable or unsure we may resort to using aggressive, manipulative or passive behaviour. (Manipulation can be very subtle and difficult to notice.)

Assertiveness training increases the chance of our using assertive behaviour more often, especially when we most need to. Learning the skills of assertiveness enables us to change our old patterns of behaviour and to develop a more positive approach to life.

Changing the way we respond to others can be exciting and stimulating. It is important to share these changes with those close to us, as this helps them to feel included, rather than threatened by the changes.

This provides the opportunity to develop self-awareness and insight into your own and theirs' behaviour.

Victim to Victor – taking our power back

Contrary to what you may have heard, learning to be assertive isn't about becoming stroppy and aggressive. Courses teach you how to deal with others so you and the person you're talking to feel good. The idea is to distinguish between blame and responsibility to analyse a situation rather than rush into blaming yourself and to handle firmly but respectfully other people (who may be trying to blame you).

When I did the course (and I would suggest it is a good idea) I was with a group of women who all had the same problem. Saying 'no' clearly and expressing what they wanted. Perhaps the biggest blame trigger in the world is being asked to do something and refusing. How to say 'no' that leave you feeling blame-free?

We paired up and were instructed just to refuse whatever the other requested. 'Can you water my plants while I am away?' 'No.'

And then to make it worse we were not allowed to say why! Make some half-hearted excuse that one was too busy, was away yourself, having an operation, anything. We just had to say 'No' and it was difficult.

After the course I worked out what I wanted to say in advance and wrote it down. Sometimes I emailed someone or put a note through their door. I did not feel this was a cop out as in the note I was making a point of not blaming the other person but just stating my own point.

I had a neighbour upstairs who put his washing on very early before he went to work and I put the note through his door explaining that I could hear the machine which woke me up. He was upset with himself, he had no idea that the machine had woken me, and the early rumble stopped. It took me a while to be able to say 'No' without making an excuse, I still do.

WORD POWER

Words to Avoid	Preferred Words
But	AND
Can't	I WILL
Could	CAN
Expect	(Implies Obligation)
Failed	Didn't succeed yet!
Forget	Remember
Help (helpless)	Assist

Hope	I Will
Maybe	When
Should	Shall
Sorry	Apologise not needed
Try	I will do my best
Would	I will

When in doubt you can always say NO!

OWNING OUR FEELINGS

This involves taking responsibility for acknowledging our feelings and how we act on them.

Feelings are both physical and emotional sensations within our body. We can learn to identify what we feel from different body clues, like a lump in the throat or butterflies in the stomach.

It is unhelpful to think of feelings as either 'bad' or 'good', as this can lead us to repress and deny those we consider to be negative.

Disclosing our feelings openly and honestly can enhance the quality of all our relationships.

Avoid blaming others for our feelings: Instead of "You make me feel angry", say "I feel angry when " This indicates that we are taking responsibility for the way we feel.

Bottling up our feelings can be destructive. We need to learn ways to physically and mentally releasing them.

People are not mind-readers – we need to tell them how we feel.

THE TOOL KIT

Setting the scene – This is to help you feel in control in the situation. Choose the time and place. Clarify what you want to say. Decide what you would like from the situation.

Disclosing Feelings – Use I' statements, own your feelings: e.g. 'I feel angry,' 'I feel happy.' Take responsibility for how you feel; avoid blaming others.

Be clear – Use short, clear statements. Avoid unnecessary padding. Be concise, specific speech.

Stay with it – Stay with your statement. Avoid getting hooked or side-tracked.

Empathising – In order to respect we need to empathise with the other person. Acknowledge that you have heard what the other person has said.

Working for a Compromise – Both parties' needs to be met. Assertiveness in not a matter of winning. Compromise leaves both parties feeling good.

This is the art of thinking positively about ourselves and our lives.

Negative thoughts lead to negative behaviour.

Try challenging your self put-downs, changing them instead into positive statements.

Try and avoid using 'imperatives' such as : I SHOULD, I OUGHT, I MUST

Replace them with words that imply choice: I COULD, I WANT TO, I CAN IF I CHOOSE.

We need to think assertively before we can behave assertively.

SELF-RESPECT

Behaving assertively demonstrates that we value ourselves.

Each time we behave assertively our self-respect rises.

Accepting ourselves as we are is more productive than constantly comparing ourselves with other people.

When things go wrong in our lives we need to remind ourselves that we are worthwhile.

Demonstrating respect for ourselves leads to gaining respect from others.

Disclose your positive feelings – give compliments to others.

Learning to 'let in' the compliments we are given increasing our self-esteem.

Accept a compliment gracefully – check that you are not throwing it back in someone's face.

Taking the risk of trying something new is a good way to building self-respect.

Things we are good at and things we could improve – learn life skills

Fake it until you make it!

When assertiveness is done properly there is no blame or judgment.

There is no guilt from you or from them.

You have stated your feelings and they will accept that.

You have the right to your own feelings.

You are good enough exactly as you are.
You will learn a lot more from these websites:

www.thewellnesssociety.org

www.getselfhelp.co.uk

Chapter 9: Bach Flower Remedies And Australian Bush Flower Essences

Dr Edward Bach – 1886 – 1936.

Dr Bach was a British Doctor, bacteriologist, homeopath and spiritual writer, best known for developing the Bach Flower Remedies, a form of alternative medicine inspired by homeopathy.

In 1930 aged 43 having worked in London hospitals he decided to start on a dedicated search for more natural and gentle healing techniques. He believed that he would find the solution to illness in nature.

He moved to Wales and discovered preparing flower remedies simply by floating petals of wild flowers in spring water. He believed that the healing petals of the plant in the early sunshine passing through water would transfer the healing power into the water.

Bach claimed it was the pattern of energy of the flower that healed based on his perceived psychic connection to the plant.

He postulated that illness was the result of a conflict between the purpose of the soul and the personality actions and outlook. An internal war leads to an emotional imbalance and energetic blockage or lack of harmony.

I started studying Bach remedies when I moved from Wales and finished my practitioner course at

Mount Vernon the Bach Center in Oxfordshire where he eventually settled.

As I parked up and walked down the bridle path I found this wonderful peaceful haven, Dr Bach's home.

We had just started on the first day when suddenly a woman from the office rushed in. There had been a terrible disaster. Airplanes had hit the Twin Towers in New York, the material capital of the western World and many people had died.

There was an American lady sitting behind me and she told me that her brother worked in the Twin Towers. We were all in shock – as was the World.

As I left that day I thought how much the World needed Dr Bach's remedies. The Rescue Remedy particularly which deals with shock and trauma.

"The real peace of the Soul and mind is with us when we are making spiritual advances, and it cannot be obtained by the accumulation of wealth alone, no matter how great." said Dr Bach.

The American lady eventually managed to reach her family to find that her brother had been late into work that day and so he survived.

Dr Bach's remedies are a simple system of healing using wild flowers.He says "As the flowers heal our fears, our anxieties, our worries, our faults and our failings, it is these we must seek, and then the disease (or emotional problem) no matter what it is, will leave us."

That simple? He says, "It is it's simplicity, combined with its all-healing effects, that is so wonderful". He goes on to say, "This system of healing, which has been Divinely revealed unto us, shows that it is our fears, our cares, our anxieties and such like that open the path to the invasion of illness."

So how does it work?

There are 38 flower remedies and each one have a positive reaction to negative thought. He suggests we first determine the personality and temperament, fears, worries, emotional unset and the subsequent effect in outlook and attitude.

The 38 remedies are placed under 7 headings:

For Fear -Rock Rose, Mimulus, Cherry Plum, Aspen, Red Chestnut

For Uncertainly -Cerato, Scleranthus, Gentian, Gorse, Hornbeam, Wild Oat

For Insufficient Interest in Present Circumstances - Clematis, Honeysuckle, Wild Rose, Olive, White Chestnut, Mustard, Chestnut Bud

For Loneliness – Water Violet, Impatience, Heather

For Over-sensitivity to Influences and Ideas – Agrimony, Centaury, Walnut, Holly,

For Despondency or Despair – Larch, Pine, Elm, Sweet Chestnut, Star of Bethlehem, Willow, Oak, Crab Apple,

For Over-Care for Welfare of Others -Chicory, Vervain, Vine, Beech, Rock Water,

These days most Bach Flower Remedy books are in alphabetical order so in the Appendix I will explain each remedy with description and the positive outcome. There are several flowers which are good for worry and I have put a star next to them. Two stars for the remedies which are also in Rescue Remedy – wonderful for any emergency.

In our search for the hero this is a good place to start.

In Judy Howard book 'The Bach Flower Remedies step by step' she says: "The remedies healing energies simply lift our vibrations and unblock the channels within our minds so that we can approach life more positively. And with the return of inner strength and harmony, the body's own natural healing processes are able to begin."

The Flower remedies struck a chord with me as soon as I heard of them. They are almost the only gentle and natural form of healing that helps the emotions and are pain free. Having encountered a lot of painful procedures I found the idea very appealing, and no side effects! The remedies are very subtle and it may act quickly or slowly.

They do not take the place of modern medicine but treat the emotions, so are unique.

I had a client, my Reiki Master who had lost his wife after a long illness. Although her death was expected when it came he was shocked as she seemed to be improving. He found when he did Reiki with clients his nose would run, making the sessions difficult, he also had nose bleeds which he had been having for about 6 years.

I gave him various remedies as it was obvious to me that he was suffering from shock. So I gave him Star of Bethlehem, Mimulus for known fears as he had financial worries. Then Holly as he was angry with his daughter who had disposed of his wife's ashes (he had not been able to cope with at the time). He was an easy going type but lonely so Agrimony was needed. Finally Beech as he was intolerant towards his family.

After a week he rang me and told me that he was totally well. His nose drip had stopped as had the nose bleeds. He wanted to tell his specialist what had happened and how wonderful it was not to suffer any more.

There are many wonderful Flower Essence makers around the World now. I have been lucky enough to study under some of them. My favourite is the Bush Essences from Australia.

Ian White the creator of the remedies is very much alive and inspiring people around the World.

Ian White says that the Australian Bush Essence remedies are catalysts to unlock your full potential, resolve negative beliefs and bring about harmony. Australian plants have a real beauty and strength. There is something remarkable about them. Not only does Australia have the highest number of flowering plants, they are also the oldest in the world.

I have found his Remedies and Combination Essences very powerful and have had a lot of success for myself and my clients. Find out more in the Appendix.

Flower remedies are good for animals too and when I was on one of Ian White's courses I asked him about my old horse who was giving me cause to worry. My horse was depressed I could tell, had lost a bit of his spark and the vet said was getting cataracts. Not a good prognosis for an old animal.

Ian suggested "Sunshine Wattle" for those expecting a grim future, the positive outcome being 'open to a bright future'.

I started putting drops in his feed. He needed more drops than a human so I doubled the dose.

As time went on and I becoming progressively incapacitated by arthritis I decided it would be better for him to go to the riding for the disabled who had offered him a place. He would be surrounded by children (which he loved). Bearing that in mind I got him vetted again.

It was a new vet who explained that he could find no fault with his eyes at all. With a clean bill of health I sent him off to finish his life happily carrying small children on his back.

You can find out more about the Australian Bush Flower Essences at:
www.ausflowers.com.au

For Bach sites:
www.bachcentre.com
www.healingherbs.co.uk

Chapter 10: Breath Techniques

The Power of Breath

The first thing we do as we are born is breathe and the last thing when we die. Yet because it is automatic it's easy to take it for granted.

Few people are fully aware when their breathing rate and rhythm changes, especially when they are under stress. Yet Andrew Weil, MD, states that conscious breathing is the most important thing we can do for our health, regardless of exercise and diet.

This is an amazing statement.

Breathing techniques have always been a part of meditation, martial arts, yoga and other healing modalities. In western civilization there has been little awareness of the power of breath until recently, when used as part of stress management programs and some alternative work.

Benefits of all breathing techniques:

Anxiety reduced

High stress level reduction

Deep relaxation

Increased energy

Emotional stability

Improvement of health

Enhancement of the immune system

Inner peace

Develop greater spiritual awareness

Here are some short breathing techniques that you can easily practice throughout the day.

<small>Technique for Anxiety</small>

1.This breathing exercise acts as a natural tranquilizer for the nervous system. Perform this exercise sitting with straight back. Place and keep your tongue behind the upper front teeth. Completely exhale through your mouth making a 'woosh' sound. Close and inhale through your nose. Count 4. Hold to count of 7. Exhale through your mouth. Continue until you are calmer.

If you are in the situation in public and panic skip 1. and don't worry about the 'woosh' if you will be embarrassed.

2. Box Breathing – simple to learn and do. Exhale to the count of 4. Hold your lungs empty for the count of 4. Inhale to the count of 4. Hold the air in your lungs for 4. Exhale and begin the pattern again.

3. Simple Breathing. This exercise can be done at any time and repeated as often if needed. Inhale slowly through your nose. Relax shoulders. Concentrate on your abdomen which should expand. Your chest should raise very little.

Exhale through your mouth. As you blow the air out relax your jaw. Do the exercise until you feel calmer.

TECHNIQUE FOR STIMULATING THE BREATHING

Although we tend to associate conscious breathing with relaxation, sometimes we need to increase energy, and this is where the stimulating breath is helpful if feeling sluggish physically or mentally.

Sit in a comfortable position, loosen clothes if tight. Touch your tongue to the roof of your month just above front teeth. Breathe rapidly in and out of the nose, keeping mouth closed. Length of the inhale and exhale should be equal. Practice initially for 15 seconds, gradually increasing to a minute.

Use whenever you want to feel energised.

TECHNIQUE FOR RELAXATION

Breath Reversal – In this technique we are reversing the breath. Start focusing on the breath cycle with the exhalation. Consciously exhale contracting your muscles emptying your lungs Inhale, you will find it is fuller.

Extended Exhale – The Vagus nerve in the chest is a major component to help us relax. This nerve sends information to the brain to change the breathing pattern. You can control this by exhaling longer than inhale. Practice counting to two inhaling and then four to exhaling.

TECHNIQUE FOR MEDITATION

Focus on the Abdomen. Close your eyes and allow your body to relax. I suggest you sit in a comfortable chair. Then gently focus your awareness on the movement of your abdomen as you breath in and out. Clear your mind and simply continue focusing on your abdomen. When you become aware of your mind wandering gently bring it back to your awareness of your abdomen.

Continue from 5 to 15 minutes.

Breath Awareness Meditation

Close your eyes and allow your body to relax. Focus your awareness on your nostrils, at the place where the breath enters and exits. Stay with that focus. When you become aware of your mind wandering bring it back to focus on your nostrils.

Continue for 5 to 15 minutes.

Breath Counting Meditation

Close your eyes and allow your body to relax. Breathe in gently and as you breathe out think 'one'. Breathe in gently. As you breathe out, think 'two'. Breathe in gently. As you breathe out, think 'three'. Breathe in gently.

Continue and repeat for 5 to 15 minutes.

These are just a few exercises for you to practice if needed. You will find a lot more on line at www.verywellmind.com

Chapter 11: The Emotional Ladder

I first heard about the Emotional Ladder from a writer called Gill Edwards. Her book 'Living Magically' was the first book I bought after my partner died. I just walked into a book shop and took it off the shelf without thinking. It was the first time I did something spontaneously, completely on my own, and it felt good.

At that point I was still in shock and grieving so looking at the Emotional Ladder gave me meaning. I was at the bottom and could see how far I had to go. I was determined to get there.

I still believed at that point that my big love would blossom. But slowly I saw that it would not. The suicide of my partner was too much for the other man but it took me time to see that; maybe two years. Then I saw that unrequited love had kept me alive, it had given me meaning at a time when I needed it. I was starting to climb the ladder.

In Gill Edwards book 'Life is a Gift' she says that: "Feelings are the language of the Soul. The Universe offers emotional guidance so that you can feel your way back into the flow – but it cannot send you new and happy conditions if you are thinking the same old fearful, guilt-ridden, despairing or resentful thoughts. Nothing changes until you do".

She suggests that: Nothing can block you except your resistance. You get what you focus upon. Feel your way into the flow of your emotions. Self-awareness is the key – Look Within. The great news is that we live in an energy-based reality. You only need to change your thoughts and you begin to attract new reality.

You are not dependent upon anyone or anything 'out there' changing."

THE EMOTIONAL LADDER

Love, joy, passion, trust, gratitude, enthusiasm, clarity, freedom, intuitive knowing, empowerment
Happiness, optimism
Hope, contentment
Pessimism, boredom
Frustration, irritation, impatience
Overwhelm, worry, disappointment, doubt
Blame, anger, control, self-righteousness
Hate, rage, envy, jealousy, obsession
Guilt, insecurity, feel unworthy, self-sacrifice, feel trapped or controlled
Fear, grief, depression, disempowerment, despair

High vibration

Lower vibration

In Deb Shapiro's book "Your body speaks your mind" she says: "You are in charge of your own attitudes and feelings, of the way you treat yourself and your world, but you cannot determine the outcome of every circumstance, just as you do not make the sun rise or set, keep the earth in orbit, or make the rain fall. You are responsible for developing peace of mind. The resolution and healing of your inner being is within your control, and this may also bring a cure to the physical body"

Because of my Arthritis I started to look at the connection between my emotions and my body and found a connection straight away.

When I was rejected by the new man my knees swelled so badly that I had to go to bed. I determined to stay there until I could find out why? When I thought love was mine I felt so well, even when I was with him my body felt wonderful. So it became obvious, being in love I felt well, rejection and depression caused swelling and pain in my knees.

But why? I had only loved him! Then I saw someone in my life, my mother who had always loved me and all I had given her was rejection.

So I got out of bed and went down to see her. I told her I loved her, even though it was one of the most difficult thing I had ever done.

I had climbed that ladder, or rather I had just taken a step.

My knees returned to their usual size and I was able to continue with my life. Looking for meaning in my life had just started.

Climbing the Emotional Ladder is about shedding the old negative thoughts and beliefs we have about ourselves. Look for the good in yourself and others and you can't go wrong.

Look at the bad in the self and others and down you go.

Any way you can take action in a positive way. Even anger will give us the impetus to take action and move up the ladder. (For instance blame will not do it – that's just going down the ladder and you may get stuck.)

The ladder is about emotions and it's also about energy. When we are happy we have more of it, when depressed we can't be bothered and have less of it.

So you are improving your life by becoming more energised and positive. Life is bound to improve and happiness is in reach.

For instance: Why do we get angry?

Christopher Boyce says: 1. We get angry if someone does something that we don't want them to do.

2. Or we get angry if someone doesn't do what we want them to do.

Travel back into your life, remember a few times when you got angry, you will soon realise that you were angry at 1 or 2 reasons.

Unfortunately, your triggered angry responses are unconsciously created, and you have very little control over them. Anger is built into all of us, including animals, it is designed to Keep us safe, it's what is called the Fight or Flight response.

Warranted Anger, as in the example of a ferocious dog, the fight or flight response anger is acceptable, it's our built-in defense mechanism.

Unwarranted Anger you have a puppy, not yet fully toilet trained. You notice a wet patch on the carpet, and you get angry and scold it. The puppy hasn't done what you want it to do.

How to fix it:

Once unwarranted anger has arrived at the forefront of your mind it's only then can you deal with it. Unwarranted anger comes from a choice, we can choose how to respond to an event, and we can either be angry or not angry about it.

Warranted Anger – say you see someone pushing in front of a queue and that triggers anger within you. But not everyone in the queue is angry with this. Why? It is likely because they have not chosen to be angry about it. And you can do the same, you can choose to be angry, or you can choose not to be angry. What is important to understand is this: Whether you are angry or not angry about an event, the event won't change, but you have the free will how you respond to an event, and that is the secret.

The hero climbs to the top knowing that nothing is more important than feeling good.

The choices made decide what kind of life lived.

The Hero has free will and knows that a positive response to life can bring joy and love.

Websites:

www.superioetics.com
www.livingmagically.com

Chapter 12: Forgiveness

We have talked about or touched on Forgiveness earlier in the text but I feel it is worth putting some time looking into why we don't let go of the past and why it let's us effect our lives – sometimes in a negative way.

Louise L Hay says: "Forgiveness is a tricky and confusing concept for many people, but know that there's a different between forgiveness and acceptance. Forgiving someone doesn't mean that you condone their behaviour! The act of forgiveness takes place in your own mind. It really has nothing to do with the other person. The reality of true forgiveness lies in setting yourself free from pain.

Also, forgiveness doesn't mean allowing the painful behaviour actions of another to continue in life. Take a stand and setting healthy boundaries if often the best thing you can do – not only for yourself, but for the other person as well." Quote from 'Trust Life', Published by Hay House on 2nd Oct 2018.

She goes on to say that you can choose to:
Stay stuck and resentful or take a chance and letting it go. Seeing your experience as not your identity. It does not define yourself. Do yourself a favour and be willing to forgive. Move on to create a joyous, fulfilling life. You have the freedom to do this. You have choice This is not the end of the story.

Louise often says that all you need is to be willing and the rest will follow. The fact that you have just considered it is a start towards forgiveness.

THE DARKENED THEATER

Sit quietly and close your eyes. Allow your mind and body to relax. Then imagine yourself sitting in a darken theater and in front of you is a small stage. On that stage place the person you resent the most. It could be someone in the past or present, living or dead.
When you see this person clearly, visualize good things happening to this person – things that would have meaning to them. See them smiling and happy.

Holding this image for a few minutes then let it fade away.

Then add another step. As this person leaves the stage put yourself up there. See good things happening to you. See yourself smiling and happy. Be aware that happiness and forgiveness is available to you.

You can repeat this with as many people as you like but always end with yourself.

Congratulate yourself, you deserve it.

Two Chairs

Choose a time when you will be alone, without the phone ringing or anyone interfering.

Put two chairs opposite each other. Sit in the most comfortable or your usual chair. Close your eyes and imagine the person who has caused you the most pain and put them in the other chair. Really see them, imagine them sitting there.

Then with eyes open start talking to them. Try and do this out loud if you can. Tell them all the things you never did say. Get out all the feelings that you have held on to and possibly never talked to them about. Even if this may seem stupid you will know what to say and express.

Once you have said everything you need to them change chairs. Sit in their chair and be that other person. Try to be them and see things from their point of view. This will help you get perspective into the situation, and you will get a better picture into their world too.

Do this for as long as feels necessary, and repeat if you find it helpful.

I would suggest that it might be useful to writing things down. Then you can look back and see how far you have come.

I wrote so many journals which eventually went to the tip. It felt the right thing at the time. A time to let go of all my anger and unhappiness. A new start.

Write a letter to someone who has caused you pain or distress. Put it all down there, everything that expresses your feelings and needs. How you wanted them to behave, how they hurt you. Don't hold back, give them everything. Then fold the letter and either burn it or bury it. Be creative with how you get rid of it.

I am suggesting that you don't send it, but if you do use positive affirmation methods and do not blame the other person. Say it from your point of view ONLY and they will understand. Not from blame.

I wrote one of these letters to the man who I felt had rejected me. I wrote lots of them. Eventually I felt I needed to make a dramatic gesture, do something drastic to help me move on.

So I climbed a very steep hill near where I lived in Wales, and it was a real struggle for me. I put the letter under the trig point at the top.

I was high up and I sat thinking about him and what I had put in the letter.

As I was sitting there an air force jet (they would practice in the valleys during the day) came very slowly past me at the same level. He saw me and I saw him. Then he was gone at high speed.

If I had been looking for a sign that was it. He was gone and I thanked him for leaving.

What would I have learnt moving from one relationship to another?

I had to thank and forgive him, he had done me a favour. He had given me a chance to change my life for the better, to be myself and not defined by another. I could move on at last.

Don't forget to Forgive YOURSELF. We can be hard on ourselves and take ourselves to task.

Forgiveness is vital. Let go of what you did, or said. It is gone now. The only one who holds on to it is you.

Remember it is your ego that can cause problems, stress, disappointment and unhappiness. Do not blame yourself. It is over and done.

But if you feel you must apologise and that it is the right thing to do say:

"If I hurt you I am sorry", or something that seems appropriate.

When you can say "I am not my past" and "I am willing to forgive my past", you can create a new future.

With forgiveness, a new chapter begins.

Websites:

www.verywellmind.com

www.pranaworld.net

Chapter 13: Meditation

"Meditation is a life time's journey along the path to yourself". I quote the words of Chris Hill a Meditation Teacher and go on mentioning some other ideas from a pamphlet she wrote.

"Meditation will quieten your mind, enhance your ability to be insightful and understanding and give you a sense of inner peace. Meditation is the way we get in touch with ourselves".

"As we journey with ourselves we can reach our own center more easily. Without constant thought, and in complete freedom, staying in the present moment. Viewing the world and ourselves from this stillness of being is to live without fear and grow in love".

"In a secular world meditation can be used as a healing therapy for stress, one pays attention to one's inner self.

"In meditation I sit, present, with myself, and can build a relationship with myself just like my best friend."

Choose a quiet part of the house or garden. Sit in a comfortable chair (or the floor if you are comfortable with that), cushions in the right place and cloths loose. The body should be erect and not slumped. An invisible line runs down the body from head to toe. This upright position

encourages an unimpeded circulation of energy contributing to wakefulness.

Eyes should be closed or half closed.

Hands in lap or on thighs.

Mouth gently closed.

Head sitting happily on top of the spine, not bent forward or back.

Breathe into your abdomen 10 times.

Then scan your body in your imagination bringing your breath into each part.

Breath into toes and slowly up through the body until you reach your face.

Set your timer if needed (start with 10 minutes)

Using either breath (or mantra*) as a focus, start your meditation.

Re-enter the room energised and refreshed!

"As we focus, the mind slows down, we become attentive and relaxed and other thoughts slip away . . . but not for long, we can't blank them out, but we can let them float away and pay them little attention. Each time we drop a thought we enjoy a moment of liberation!"

If you are concentrating on the breath, just watch it going in and out. If you have a mantra* (usually given by a guru or teacher) continue to repeat the word throughout the session your mind over and over. So when your mind wanders, bring it back gently again and again. Moments of oneness allow our body and mind to feel extremely clear and stable. The wandering mind is restless, the still mind is alert.

Benefits of Meditation

Relief from stress and hypertension

Proven change in brain waves and brain chemistry

Benefits on all level of well-being

Relief from coping with chronic pain

Provide a clear anchor of focus in life

Gives the mind time to relax and rest

There are many forms of Meditation including guided meditation. Many people enjoy to be guided and at first you may find it helpful.

In Thick Nhat Hanh book "The Blooming of the Lotus" he calls it 'guided meditation to achieving the miracle of mindfulness.'

He goes on to say that you need to practice just sitting. Keeping your breathing light and even, with you mind awake, calm and clear.

"If you sit always in expectation, you cannot be in contact or enjoy the present moment, which always contains the whole of life."

A Guided Meditation: Where am I?. Close your eyes and do the meditation relaxation as above.

Imagine you are going down in a lift. See the floors going down, down to the basement. The door pings and open. (If you are scared of lifts go down the stairs until you reach the bottom).

Now you are at the bottom keep your eyes shut and say to yourself "Where am I?" "Where is the real me?" Keep asking the question.

Don't forget to breath.

Wait quietly for the voice that says "I am here" and follow it.

You may find yourself in a garden, or on a hillside, but wherever you go the sun is shining and it shines down on you. Just for you.

Find a seat and continue to enjoy the sun on you. Then when you feel rested return slowly to the room.

It also might be helpful joining a group at first who can guide you and give you the idea of what to do.

Alternatively just give yourself some time to yourself, find a quiet spot and just sit. Give yourself time off from the everyday and relax.

In the Breath Technique chapter there are Breath Meditation which you might find helpful.

Websites:

www.verywellmind.com

www.positivepsychology.com

Chapter 14: Winning Solutions

I first heard the idea of a win-win situation from a writer called Susan Jeffers. She wrote several books about fear: "Feel the Fear and do it anyway"®, and others. She says: "One of our bigger fears that keep us from moving ahead with our lives is our difficulty in making decisions. For some reason we feel we should be perfect, and forget that we learn through our mistakes."

I hope this next section will help you moving on with your life, getting a win and something good out of any situations.

Trust in your Abilities

If you knew you could handle anything that came your way, what would you possibly have to fear? Nothing!

All you have to do is develop more trust in your own abilities.

How to do that?

Susan Jeffers goes on to say: "It is often impossible to figure out what the actual causes of negative patterns are, and even if we did know, the knowing doesn't necessarily change them.
 I believe that if something is troubling you, simply start from where you are and take the
action necessary to change it.
In this case, you know that you don't like the fact

that lack of trust in yourself is stopping you from

getting what you want out of life. Knowing this creates a very clear, even laser like, focus on what needs to be changed. You don't have to scatter your energy wondering why. It doesn't matter. What matters is that you begin now to develop trust in yourself, until you reach the point where you will be able to say:

WHATEVER HAPPENS TO ME, GIVEN ANY SITUATION,

I CAN HANDLE IT!

HOW TO FIX:

Tackle things when they arise and don't worry about the future. If necessary make a plan of action, or even several, but don't fixate on it.

We worry about failure but failure should be looked on as a LEARNING TOOL. We all make mistakes. Without failure how can we learn and move on?

Don't forget that YOUR POWER LIES IN THE PRESENT MOMENT

Not in the past which is GONE

Nor in the future which is just a DREAM

ONLY NOW CAN YOU LIVE AND ACT

Think your way out of Trouble

Christopher Boyce says: "All our actions are always preceded by our thoughts. When we have good thoughts, our resulting actions are good for us, but when our thoughts are not consistent with good thoughts, it's inevitable that our actions will have negative consequences in our lives. Inappropriate thoughts that finally led to actions that caused us suffering in some way, whether it be emotional, or physical."

HOW TO FIX:

When you are in a situation that you feel needs to change, the answer is to change your thinking. Change your thinking will inevitably change your outcome, your final action.

Say you are stuck in traffic, thinking your way out of trouble will change your planned journey along another route.

This technique can be used in so many different areas of your life. By thinking, you create new thoughts, and new thoughts create new brain neurological pathways, and new pathways will lead you to carry out better actions yourself from the original actions you had planned with negative thinking.

Persevere and in less than a few weeks, you will begin to feel different inside, you will feel you are now controlling a new pathway to a new and better action for yourself.

Try it, what have you to lose?

Take a chance

I was always getting lost! I attended a flower emedy workshop at Liphook in Hampshire. I had looked it up on the map (pre sat nav) and thought I knew where it was. I was wrong.

I went down almost every road in Liphook until I found the correct one which lead to the workshop.

We finished early because the weather took a turn for the worst. I got back to town but the main road was closed because of a fallen tree. But of course by now I knew every part of Liphook so found my way around and home quite easily.

Love your Mind

It occurred to me that if I do not love my brain and my thoughts, if I keep cursing myself, what do I get? You guessed it, more of the same.

The theory is that what we think about we attract.

When I was very ill all I could think about was how ill I felt, and that is all I got. I had to grasp the concept that to change you have to change.

The same applies to our thoughts. If we keep thinking negatively we will continue to do so.

The idea of Faking until you Make It applies here.

HOW TO FIX:

Even if you don't believe it tell yourself how wonderful your thoughts and mind is. Thank it for it's help in life and how it gets you through day after day. What would you do without it? It doesn't bear thinking about!

This is a concept that took me a while to grasp but since I have been doing it my mind has been calmer and I am happy.

I have learnt GRATITUDE for what my mind does for me.

Every Moment is Different,

The only thing that keeps our World appearing the same is

OUR THOUGHTS.

To Change your World CHANGE YOUR THOUGHTS and be GRATEFUL FOR THEM.

Visualisations for Life

In Patricia Crane's book "Ordering from the Cosmic Kitchen" she talks about visualisation:

"Visualisations are imagining, seeing, feeling, or describing something you would like to create. They bring in all of the senses along with affirmations to give your subconscious mind the experience of the reality you are creating.

Your subconscious mind doesn't know the difference between the reality 'out there' and the one you create inside, so visualisation create a new 'inner landscape' that in turn produces results on the outside. Many people say that they cannot visualise, yet they can always describe their backyard or kitchen. That is a form of visualisation."

When you get anxious and imagine everything going wrong. That is visualisation. We have discussed it all the way through this book.

So the idea now is for you visualising good things happening.

HOW TO FIX:

I want you to think of someone you know who is ill or suffering in some way, maybe from anxiety. See them clearly as they are.

Then imagine them well, looking well, being and feeling well. They are living a new happy life and you see how wonderful their life has become. Hold that idea in your mind - Why not you?

Imagine your life transformed by happiness and know that you can achieve this. It's in your grasp.

Your MIND is the most Powerful thing that you own.

Use it in a Positive Way for Good

Website: www.susanjeffers.com

Chapter 15: Ends And Beginning

So we have come to the end of this book, a book that sprang out of many things. Unrequited love, illness, war, and anxiety about the future. My life had been so sad and negative. Yet today I can sit here and say: MY LIFE HAS BEEN TRANSFORMED.

An event happened to me when I was 19 which changed my life forever.

I was at Art School in the foundation year trying to decide which way to go, which course to take in art.

A group of us went on a weekend seminar to Moor Park in Farnham. I don't remember what the seminar was about or what we talked about but there was a lot of sitting about listening to lectures.

So the seminar was over and we returned to Epsom by coach. We decanted at the clock tower and I remember stepping down to the pavement and into a new world. The sun shone down on me and through me and woke me up. I was wide awake and I knew that previously I had been asleep. A sleep walker through life. It was an awakening.

The amazing thing was that I was not alone. There was a small huddle of students on the pavement who had also woken up. We gazed at each other. This was amazing.

I had days of being totally free of fear or worry. I was just living and I felt like a super hero. Anything was possible.

Slowly over days it faded but it was a beginning and I knew that living without fear and worry was possible.

What I believe I experienced was the ability to love freely. There were no barriers between myself and others. And knowing this, the event coloured everything in my life from that day on.

Louise L Hay talks a lot about love and I have only touched a little in this book but have concentrated on the practical side. But we are all searching for it. We want to be loved as we are.

Louise L Hay says: "You don't have to earn love any more than you have to earn to breathe. You have a right to breathe ...because you exist. You have a right to be loved ...because you exist. That is all you need to know. You are worthy of your own love. Don't allow society's negative opinions, or your parents or friends, to make you think that you are not good enough. The reality of your being is that you are lovable. Accept this and know this. When you really do, you will find that people treat you as a lovable person."

Quote from 'Trust Life' Published by Hay House on 2nd Oct 2018.

I heard somewhere that when one person achieves something that others have not, then we are bound to follow. Look at Roger Bannister who ran the first four minute mile! In 1954 this seemed impossible yet it has been beaten since and will continue to do so.

They call this the Roger Bannister Effect: The Psychological Breakthrough. It goes that by crushing the 4 minutes mile mark, it allowed others to dream of the impossible.

No longer held back by this psychological barrier, swarms of runners went under the barrier and by 2021 1,663 athletes have done it.

The only power worry has over you is the power you give it.

Where one person has beaten it, then so can you.

You can beat worry, you can do it.

Appendix 1

The Bach Flower Remedies

Brief description with Positive and Negative aspects.

One * could help Anxiety. Two** which are include in the Rescue remedy.

AGRIMONY "I hide behind a smile"
Negative Condition: Mental torture Behind 'Brave Face'. Restless at night, seeks excitement. Dislikes being alone. Positive Outcome: Cheerful, can laugh at worries. A good companion. A genuine optimist.

*ASPEN "I'm haunted"
Negative Condition: Fear day or night for no reason. Terror on awakening, nightmares. Positive Outcome: Fearless, faith in love. Such desire for adventure.

BEECH "Your wrong"
Negative Condition: Intolerant, critical of others. Must have exactness, complains about others. Positive Outcome: Strong convictions, high ideals. Desire to be more tolerant with others. Understanding.

CENTAURY "I'm a door mat" Negative Condition: Weak-willed, subservient. Timid, cannot say 'no'. Positive Outcome: One who serves wisely & quietly. Can say 'no', a strong individually.

CERATO "Am I OK"? Negative Condition: Seeks advice & confirmation from others. Foolish. Talkative. Tends to imitate. Positive Outcome: Wise, intuitive, holds definite opinions. Will stick to decisions.

**CHERRY PLUM "I think I'm going mad!" Negative Condition: Fear of mind giving way. Desperate. Verge of breakdown. Fear of losing control. Positive Outcome: Calm, quiet courage. Able to retain sanity despite mental and physical torture.

CHESTNUT BUD "I haven't learnt" Negative Condition: Failure to learn from mistakes. Repeat making errors. Positive Outcome: Gains knowledge from experiences. Observant of mistakes

CHICORY "Mothers knows best" Negative Condition: Possessive – Selfish. Easily hurt and offended. Positive Outcome: Give without thought of return

**CLEMATIS "When?" Negative Condition: Dreamer – lack of interest in present. Vacant. Inattentiveness. Positive Outcome: Live interest in all things. Idealistic. Inspired but realistic.

CRAB APPLE "I hate myself " Negative Condition: Self-hatred – sense of uncleanliness. Ashamed of body. Fussy, trivial thoughts. Positive Outcome: Cleansing for mind and body. Broad minded, accepts self again.

ELM "I'm overwhelmed"
Negative Condition: Overwhelmed by responsibility. Feeling inadequate and exhausted. Not up to the job. Positive Outcome: Capable, efficient, intuitive. Positive awareness of responsibilities. Leader, decision-maker.

GENTIAN "I'm put off"
Negative Condition: Discouragement – Despondent. Easily put off when things go wrong. Positive Outcome: No failure when one's doing ones best. No obstacle or task too great

GORSE "I give up"
Negative Condition: Hopeless – Despair. Almost useless to try, sufferers. Positive Outcome: Positive faith and hope. Difficulties will be overcome.

HEATHER "I'm too talkative"
Negative Condition: Self-centred, self-concern. Obsessed with ailments, problems. Positive Outcome: Selfless, understanding personal. Willing to listen and help.

HOLLY "I'm angry"
Negative Condition: Hatred, envy, jealousy. Suspicious, aggressiveness, greed. Positive Outcome: Protection from hatred. Understanding, tolerant.

*HONEYSUCKLE "Then . . . . "
Negative Condition: Lives in the past, nostalgia. Lost in present, fear future. Positive Outcome: Past experiences laid to rest. Sees experiences of value and moves on.

HORNBEAM "I can't"
Negative Condition: Monday morning feeling.
Doubts to face and cope. Positive Outcome: Certain
of own abilities. Strength to face life.

**IMPATIENCE "I'm impatient"
Negative Condition: Irritable, impatient, nervous.
Mental tension, prefers to work alone. Positive
Outcome: Less hasty in actions and thoughts.
Relaxed, patient, tolerant

LARCH "I expect failure"
Negative Condition: Lack of confident. Convinced
of failure, even to try. Positive Outcome: Not fear of
failure or successful. Determined, capable.

*MIMULUS "I'm frightened of . . "
Negative Condition: Fear of known things, illness,
accident, poverty etc. Positive Outcome: Courage to
face trials and difficulties. Emotions completely
under control.

MUSTARD "I'm gloomy"
Negative Condition: Deep gloom with no origin.
Melancholy which comes on suddenly. Positive
Outcome: Inner serenity, stability. Joy and peace.

OAK "I fight on"
Negative Condition: Despondent but struggles on.
Overworks and hides tiredness. Positive Outcome:
Courage under all conditions. Reliable, strong,
patient.

OLIVE "I'm too tired"
Negative Condition: Complete exhaustion, no reserve of strength, fatigue of mind and body. Positive Outcome: Remedy for convalescence. Restores peace and strength.

PINE "I feel guilty"
Negative Condition: Self-reproach, guilt. Blames self for mistakes, overworks. Positive Outcome: Takes responsibility, balance attitude. Perseverance, sound judgment.

*RED CHESTNUT"I'm worried about"
Negative Condition: Anxiety for others, fearing the worse. Fearful thoughts that can harm. Positive Outcome: Ability to remain calm in emergency. Positive thoughts for others.

**ROCK ROSE "I'm terrified"
Negative Condition: Terror for accident or near escape. From spectacle of accident etc. Positive Outcome: Greater courage - willing to risk life for others. Strength of will.

ROCK WATER "I'm an idealist"
Negative Condition; Self repression and denial. Rigidity of outlook, often physical too. Positive Outcome: High ideals – a flexible mind. Willing to change, be flexible.

SCLERANTHUS "I can't decide"
Negative Condition: Uncertainty, indecision, extreme varying moods. Positive Outcome: Calmness, takes prompt action/decisions. Good for sickness. Keeps poise and balanced

**STAR OF BETHLEHEM "I'm still shocked"
Negative Condition: Shock in any form, an accident, sad news, delayed shock. Positive Outcome: Neutralise shock and effects of shock immediate or delayed.

*SWEET CHESTNUT "I have come to the end"
Negative Condition: Extreme anguish, mental despair. Anguish of bereavement. Positive Outcome: Full control of emotions, stronger character. Keeps troubles to self.

VERVAIN "I'm right"
Negative Condition: Tenseness - hyper. Highly strung, fanatic. Positive Outcome: Willing to defend a cause. Calm, wise and tolerant.

VINE "Do as I do"
Negative Condition: Dominates, craves power, ruthless. Knows best. Positive Outcome: An understanding leader. Inspires and helps others.

WALNUT "I'm tempted"
Negative Condition: Protection from change and outside influences. Easily dominated. Positive Outcome: Protection from outside influences. Ideals and ambitions.

WATER VIOLET "I'm a loner"
Negative Condition: Proud, aloof, disdainful and condescending. Mental rigid. Positive Outcome: Independent and self-reliant. Sympathetic and wise.

*WHITE CHESTNUT "I can't stop thinking"
Negative Condition: Unwanted thoughts, mental argument. Thoughts going round and round in the mind. Positive Outcome: A quiet calm mind – at peace with self. Able to control thoughts.

WILD OAT "I don't know where I'm going"
Negative Condition: Uncertain of path in life. Things not clear in life's directions. Positive Outcome: Definite character, talent and ambition. Help in looking forward

WILD ROSE "I can't be bothered"
Negative Condition: Resignation, apathy, drifter. Always weary, lack in vitality. Positive Outcome: Ambitious, purposeful, interest in life. Enjoys friendships and happiness.

WILLOW "Poor me"
Negative Condition: Resentment, bitterness, self-pity. Blames everyone except self. Positive Outcome: - Optimism and faith - Takes Responsibility For Life.

These are only a brief description of the remedies. To learn more and more products

look at the website:

www.bachcentre.com

**RESCUE REMEDY

If you have a shock of any kind, some sudden bad news, a family upset, any kind of panic or terror Rescue Remedy will come to your aid. It comes in various forms and I keep a tin of Rescue capsules in my handbag to suck in times of need. I also keep a bottle of Rescue by my bed to help me sleep. You can now buy Rescue Night and also Rescue Cream which includes the 5 flower remedies. You can buy all of these from good chemists or on line.

METHOD OF DOSAGE

Take 2 drops from each chosen stock remedy in a cup of water, fruit juice, or any beverage, and sip fairly frequently. Replenish cup to continue treatment if need be. ALTERNATIVELY you can put the drops in a bottle of approx. 1 fl. oz. (30ml) capacity and fill up with Natural Spring Water (non-gas) and take 4 drops on the tongue directly from bottle. Take as often as needed but at least 4 times a day, especially first and last thing daily. Prepared dosage bottle will remain fresh for about 3 weeks but to preserve add a teaspoon of brandy or cider vinegar.

Try to limit your choices to maximum 6 remedies. Too many remedies may cloud the issue.

The remedies will help us to feel more optimistic and thus give us hope and lift our spirits.

Appendix 2

Harnessing the healing power of The Australian Bush Flower Essences

Combination Essences

EMERGENCY: Help to sooth and create balance when you need it most. It has a calming effect.

BOOST: Help to support and boost yourself through changing and challenging times.

CARERS: Supports the caregiver when they feel overwhelmed by responsibility of looking after another.

ABUND: Aids in releasing negative beliefs, family patterns, sabotage, and poverty consciousness.

ADOL: Address the major issues teenagers commonly experience.

BODY BEAUTIFUL: Acknowledge, celebrating and nurture who you are.

CALM AND CLEAR: Helps to find time for one's self, to relax even with external pressure and demands.

CONFIDENT: Bring out the positive qualities of self esteem and confidence

CREATIVE: Inspire creativity and emotional expression and gives courage clarity in public speaking and singing.

DYNAMIS: Renews enthusiasm and joy for life.

ELECTRO: Helps release uncomfortable feelings associated with earth, electricity and electromagnet radiation.

FOCUS: Gives clarity and focus when working, speaking, reading or studying.

MEDITATION: Awakens one's spirituality and allows one to go deeper into any religious or spiritual practice.

MEN'S: For men always on the go which can lead to impatience or irritation.

PURIFYING: To assist with the release and cleansing of emotions waste and residue by-products, to clear built-up emotional baggage.

RELATIONSHIP: Enhances the quality of all relations especially intimate ones.

SEXUAL: Helpful for releasing negative experiences associated with one's sexuality.

SOLARIS: For uncomfortable emotional feelings associated with heat, fire or sun.

TRANSITION: Helps one to cope and move through any major life change.

TRAVEL: Helps you arrive refreshed, balanced and ready to go.

WOMAN: It allows a woman to discover and feel good about herself, her body and her beauty.

SPACE CLEARING: Great for clearing tense situations and environment and restore balance.

SENSUALITY: Encourage the ability to enjoy emotionally intimacy.

Taking the Remedies: Seven drops under the tongue morning and night.

There are 69 individual remedies of the Australian Bush Essences and many of them are included in the Combination Essences.

If you have an individual problem I would advise approaching the website for help as every remedy has a specific meaning.

You can buy the essences individually and if you make them up yourself follow the advise as per Bach but instead of 2 drops per bottle add 7.

As the Combination Essences take morning and night.

Look at the website for more products and advice. www.ausflowers.com.au

The essences will help us unlock our full potential, resolve negative beliefs and bring about harmony.

Glossary

"A Course in Miracles"
ISBN: 978-1-883360-26-9

"Heal Thyself" by Dr Edward Bach
ISBN:0-85207-301-1

"Dictionary of the Bach Flower Remedies" by TW
Hyne Jones
ISBN:0-85207-145-0

"The Bach Flower Remedies, Step by Step" by Judy
Howard
ISBN:0-85207-223-6

"Ordering from the Cosmic Kitchen" by Patricia J
Crane
ISBN:1-893705-15-3

"How to Interpret your Dreams" by Pierre Daco
ISBN:1-85487-668-6

"Living Magically", by Gill Edwards
ISBN:0-7499-1074-7

"Life is a Gift", by Gill Edward
ISBN:978-0-7499-2781-3

"The Blooming of a Lotus" by Thich Nhat Hanh
ISBN:0-8070-1237-8

"You can Heal your Life" by Louise L Hay
ISBN:0-937611-01-8

"Trust Life" by Louise L Hay
ISBN:978-1-78817-305-6

"Feel the Fear and Do it Anyway"®, by Susan Jeffers
ISBN:0-7126-7105-6

"The Body Speaks Your Mind", by Deb Shapiro
ISBN:0-7499-2783-6

"62 Australian Bush Flowers", by Ian White
ISBN:0-646-28403-7

"Bush Flower Healing", by Ian White
ISBN:0-73380-053-X

"Bush Flower Essences", by Ian White
ISBN:0-905249-84-4

"Teach only Love", by Gerald G Jampolsky, MD
ISBN:1-58270-033-8

About the Author

Marian Foss was born in Edinburgh in 1950. A baby boomer, in the 60's she became a hippy and embraced the culture of sex, drugs and rock and roll. Their ideal was to change the world for the better with Peace and Love.

She attended Epsom Art School and left with a Dip Ad in Art and Design.

Then worked in Advertising and Television for companies such as the BBC, Channel 4, Thames TV and Decca Records.

In 1990 she was told that she would not be able to work again due to long term Rheumatoid Arthritis, a crippling and painful disease.

A dramatic turn in events helped her realize that she needed to change direction and for the last 25 years she has been studying and training in many Alternative Therapies and now is an Advanced Louise L Hay Teacher, Reiki Master, Bach Flower Practitioner and Healing Breath work trainer. Recently she returned to Painting.

She would describe herself as a Modern Mystic.

"I have come to realize that with every dis-ease comes anxiety. Our body is out of control and we are constantly trying to put it right. It was like that for me. But you don't need to be ill to have worry, it's something anyone can suffer from.

In this book I hope that I have explained how worry works and how to be free of it. It has certainly worked for me. I have also included all the alternative therapies I have studied in part 3.

It's possible to turn life around as I have and if one person can do it so can you. This is your journey but take heart and know that it is possible. I can just point you in the right direction."

www.whyworry.org.uk